The Windrush Scandal: The History of the Modern Controversy and Race Relations in the British Empire

By Charles River Editors

The HMT *Empire Windrush*

About Charles River Editors

Charles River Editors is a boutique digital publishing company, specializing in bringing history back to life with educational and engaging books on a wide range of topics. Keep up to date with our new and free offerings with this 5 second sign up on our weekly mailing list, and visit Our Kindle Author Page to see other recently published Kindle titles.

We make these books for you and always want to know our readers' opinions, so we encourage you to leave reviews and look forward to publishing new and exciting titles each week.

Introduction

Theresa May

"Migration was not a word I would have used to describe what I was doing when I sailed with other West Indians to England in 1950. We simply thought we were going to an England that had been painted in our childhood consciousness as a heritage and a place of welcome. It is the measure of our innocence that neither the claim of heritage nor the expectation of welcome would have been seriously doubted. England was not for us a country with classes and conflicts of interest like the islands we left. It was the name of a responsibility whose origin may have coincided with the beginning of time." – George Lamming, *In the Castle of My Skin*

On the morning of June 22, 1948, the HMT *Empire Windrush*, a repurposed German troopship, drew up alongside the Tilbury docks, lowering its gangplanks onto the wide, cobbled quays. To the casual interest of the dockworkers, a small army of well-dressed, luggage laden blacks stepped onto the shores of England, looking around for the first time at their new home. Most originated from Kingston, the capital of the British island colony of Jamaica, with a few others from Trinidad and a handful of other British Caribbean dependencies. These were the men and women who led the vanguard of what would come to be known as the *Windrush Generation*, the first substantial wave of non-white immigration to the British Isles from the outer marches of the Empire. Ultimately, between 1948 and 1970, more than half a million souls would migrate to the United Kingdom from the Caribbean and other non-white Commonwealth countries, establishing the bedrock of the British black community and prompting the first ripples of racial discomfort that would conclude in the infamous Windrush Scandal of 2018.

The issue of race in the British Empire is as complex as the history of the British Empire itself. The origins of the British Empire lie in the settlement of North America and the Caribbean, both of which led to complex intersections of imperialism, commerce and race. While the first European encounters with the New World were Spanish, the British arrived on the scene in a permanent way with the establishment of a General Assembly of the Leeward Islands in 1674, after which, in a complex evolution in competition and conflict with other European trading powers, the British West Indies finally comprised the British Leeward Islands, the British Windward Islands, Jamaica, and other colonies such as the Cayman Islands, British Honduras and the Turks and Caicos Islands. The Caribbean was colonized for reasons both economic and strategic, the former being the seedbed of the institution that would define the demographics of the region up to the present and impact race relations back in Britain as well.

The Windrush Scandal: The History of the Modern Controversy and Race Relations in the British Empire examines how racism in the United Kingdom affected the empire at home and abroad. Along with pictures of important people and places, you will learn about the Windrush Scandal like never before.

Racism and Colonialism

   Slavery took root in the Caribbean almost at the moment that Columbus claimed Hispaniola for Spain. Once the native Tainos and Arawak communities had been destroyed through a combination of disease and slavery, the first African slaves began arriving, establishing a trade that would ensure the profitability of the region, but which would also create cultural reverberations that tend now to define the modern age. Slavery already defined the role and popular perception of the black races in the eyes of most other participating races in the era of global expansion. Throughout the era of slavery, the prevailing view of black Africans in the Arab world, in particular after the rise of Islam, was as slaves, a subservient race, the residue of which lingers most notably today in the attitude of Islamic Sudan to Christian-animist South Sudan. Under the canons of Islamic law, the institution of slavery was codified and regulated, bringing into civilized discourse a phenomenon as ancient as human society itself. The Mameluke, for example, a slave caste, its origins set deep in the history of the Caucuses, rose to rule Egypt under the Ottomans, their origins as slaves worn as a mark of curious distinction. Lost in deep history is the Egyptian tradition of employing Nubian slaves as the fighting men of the empire, their women as concubines, and eunuchs in the employ of sultans to protect the sanctity of their harems.

   As one considered the case of the British Empire, however, the tale of Dadabhai Naoroji and Mohandas Gandhi perhaps best defines the curious admixture of racial attitudes that characterized that institution. For gernations, the flagship British imperial possession was India, control of which was gained by increments from 1600 onwards. Before 1858, the colony was administered by the British East India Company, subject to guidance from a desk at the Foreign Office, and administered by various gubernatorial appointments. Generations of mounting economic malfeasance and exploitation came to a head in 1857 with the mutiny of a handful of regiments of the Indian Army. The Indian Army at that time was a private force maintained by the Company comprising indigenous rank and file led by a corps of British officers and senior non-commissioned officers. The mutiny was a close-run thing, with the fate of the British in India balancing on a knife's edge as the loyalty of the bulk of the regimental structure was tested. While in the end the revolt was put down by loyal Indian troops and as the local administration breathed a deep sigh of relief, the British imperial government was forced at last to acknowledge that things could not continue as they were.

   Both the limitations and fitness of a private company to rule a nation of 300 million people were pushed to the forefront of the national debate, prompting a wide-ranging revision of government and administration in India. The horse-trading and policy construction that went into this transition does not directly concern us here, other than to remark that, according to the terms of the Government of India Act of 1858, the British East India Company ceded control, handing over the administration of the colony to the British Imperial Government. Thereafter, with an august history spanning almost three centuries, the British East India Company faded into obscurity, disappearing entirely in 1874. Queen Victoria added "Empress of India" to her titles, and in the afterglow of the creation of the British Raj, a Royal Proclamation was issued that defined for the first time the relationship between the sovereign monarch of the British Empire and her subjects.

The full title of the document was "Proclamation, by the Queen in Council, to the Princes, Chiefs and People of India," wherein a promise was made to the traditional rulers of India, the old "Princely States" that had for long governed under the principle of indirect rule, albeit subject to British overlordship, that Her Majesty's government would protect their sovereignty in political and religious matters. Many of these princes and traditional leaders were hangovers from the glorious days of the Mughal Empire, and most were Islamic. More importantly than this was a solemn promise to all subjects of the British Crown "of whatever race or creed, be freely and impartially admitted to offices in our service, the duties of which they may be qualified, by their education, ability, and integrity, duly to discharge…"

The implications of this were that all British subjects in any territory flying the Union Jack enjoyed equal opportunity, freedom of travel, full franchise rights, religious liberty and equality under the law. This defined the relationships of the various constituent colonies, protectorates and territories of the British Empire with one another and with Britain, and the rights of each and all residents within, defined under the simple principle of equality.

The Proclamation, however, did not alter the overarching system of government in India, which remained a British colony under the direct administration of the Crown through the offices of a Viceroy and various regional governors. Within this system, Indian subjects were not independent and enjoyed only minimal representation within their borders. The first to challenge and explore the outer limits of this new liberal mindset was a certain Parsi academic by the name of Dadabhai Naoroji.

Naoroji

As a pale-skinned Parsi, Naoroji was perhaps less of a challenge to British institutionalized racism than might have been a darker-skinned Indian or an African. He was Zoroastrian, of ancient Persian origin, and a highly accomplished scholar and academic. Besides serving as professor of Mathematics and Natural Philosophy at the Elphinstone College in Bombay, and later of Gujarati language and history at the University College London, he held various local political offices and was one of the founding members of the Indian Congress Party.

A moderate in every sense of the word, Naoroji was among a large number of high-born and educated Indians who revered the British, acknowledged the gifts that the British had endowed on India, both materially and morally, and reveled in inclusion among the British noble classes. However, he also rankled under an insufferable, paternalistic system of government that limited the ability of Indians to control their own destiny and govern their own affairs. There was no particular movement at that time to oust the British from India, but simply to curb the worst of their excesses, and to lift to some degree the suffocating burden of foreign rule.

How Naoroji chose to illustrate this point remains one of the great chapters of race history in the British Empire. Under the terms of the Royal Proclamation of 1858, as noted above, any subject of Her Majesty enjoyed the right to enter into political office anywhere in the Empire regardless of race, color or creed. In 1888, to test this truth, Naoroji sold his interests in India, resigned his tenure at Elphinstone, and travelled to London where he established himself in academia and prepared to enter politics.

He joined the Liberal Party and campaigned for the parliamentary seat of Finsbury Central, a middle-class constituency of North London. In large part, his objective in this was to introduce the Victorian public to the Indian elite, and to stand for office in the metropolitan capital not as a second-class Englishman, but as a first-class Indian. He was defeated only narrowly in the 1892 general election by a Tory establishment candidate, a fact that was hardly commented on by the press at all. It did, however, cause the British Prime Minister, the Marquis of Salisbury, to reflect on the matter in an address to the Scottish parliament a few weeks later. Naoroji's loss did not surprise him, he remarked, since he believed that the British electorate was not yet ready to elect to public office a "black man."

This comment, to the astonishment of the Prime Minister, provoked an uproar in the national press, the reasons for which are interesting. Naoroji was a Parsi whose complexion was as pale as the lightest Englishman, and whose political and academic accomplishments were vast. It was pointed out to the Prime Minister, in ways many and creative, that the residents of the British Isles were still warring and hunting bison in their woad paint as the Indus civilization was devising one of the first written languages, complex mathematic principles, multi-layered religion and philosophy and advanced traditions of art and architecture. To so insult a representative of one of the finest cultures in the world by publicly naming him as a "black man" hardly did justice to the British establishment, and it would not endear the Indian elites to the British in a manner that might perpetuate the partnership of empire.

The net result of this was that Naoroji was instantly projected to the forefront of the national debate, and in the following general election of 1896, he duly defeated the Tory candidate and took his seat on the backbenches. While his tenure was brief and his victory was narrow – he was thereafter nicknamed by the press "Narrow Majority" – the moment was one of enormous symbolic importance, for it illustrated unequivocally the willingness of the press and the middle classes of Victorian Britain to embrace an Indian as an equal.

In the aftermath of it all, Naoroji settled back into the rarified pursuits of academia, making his home in London. There he acted as a mentor to many young Indians arriving in the imperial capital to pursue their education, and others seeking his tutelage as the Indian independence movement began to gather pace.

One of these was a young barrister by the name of Mohandas Karamchand Gandhi. Gandhi, a minor Gujarati aristocrat, studied law at the University of London, qualified as a barrister and gained membersship in the British Bar Association. Back in India, he found himself competing in the legal system of Bombay with a small army of similarly qualified men, and briefs, as a consequence, were few and far between. He was, however, offered a contract to act as liaison and legal interpreter between a pair of feuding Gujarati businessmen in South Africa. His host and employer, a towering figure of the local Indian community, was Dada Abdulla, a long-term resident and trader in the port city of Durban, the economic capital of the British colony of Natal. The dispute, however, was with a cousin of the family who was resident in the neighboring Boer republic of Transvaal. This was a complicating factor because the Natal colony was under British administration and subject to British law, while the Transvaal was an independent republic under Boer administration.

Gandhi in 1909

Natal, being a British colony, was subject to the terms of the Royal Proclamation, meaning that an Indian national, as a subject of Her Majesty, was entitled to equality in all matters, and as a British lawyer, he deserved due full professional courtesy by the local judiciary and bar. Despite this, Gandhi's arrival in Natal created quite a considerable amount of discomfort, and while the hands of the local administration and judiciary were tied in regards to shutting him out of the system, he was certainly made welcome nowhere. Nonetheless, he was in the territory on a specific contract, and, with his customary charm, forbearance, and articulation, he navigated the worst of the petty pinpricks, looking forward all the while to leaving South Africa, never to return.

Then, as the first hearing was scheduled, he was obliged to travel to Pretoria, the capital of the Transvaal. He purchased a first-class ticket and boarded a passenger rail car bound from Durban to the Transvaal frontier, from where he would continue on by coach. Within the precincts of Durban, the sight of an Indian gentleman in a first-class compartment excited no particular comment, but as the train climbed the escarpment and drew into the town of Pietermaritzburg, it certainly did. The matter was brought to the attention of the conductor who was then obliged to inform the young lawyer that he was required to step back into third class.

Gandhi, who was already a man of decided opinions, refused, uttering something to the effect that he would yield only to force. This did not dismay the conductor, and a few minutes later, in the chill of the evening, Mohandas Gandhi found himself standing on the platform watching as the lights of the train disappeared around the bend. Thus, he passed a bitterly cold night, brooding over the matter, which he decided simply would not be allowed to stand. That moment, as many historians have been apt to remark, marked the beginning of the end of the British Empire.

Gandhi arrived eventually in Pretoria, having been forced, despite a ticket, to ride on the luggage rack of the coach, at which point he found himself in an environment of statutory racism worse in every respect than anything in Natal. The Indian community of Natal, significant by then, was the residual consequence of the indentured labor policy, that generally filled the labor vacuum in the British Empire left by the abolition of slavery. In the wake of waves of low caste Indian workers came a class of mainly Muslim traders and minor professionals, among whom was Dada Abdulla. The Transvaal Indians, on the other, comprised mainly merchants and traders from Natal who were exploiting the bonanza of the Witwatersrand, then home to the greatest and richest goldrush in history. Without regulation, and in an environment swirling with cash, Indian traders, for a brief and golden season, reaped fortunes and were quite content to live in ghettos and suffer the indignity of naked racism for so long as the going was so good.

Gandhi, however, arrived in the midst of it all with an irritated temper, and he was unwilling to let these issues pass. He ignored, for example, a civic ordinance prohibiting non-whites from walking on city sidewalks, as he did a strict curfew for non-whites after 9:00 p.m. To avoid the latter, he was granted a special pass by the Transvaal Attorney General who happened to be a member of the same bar association as he. While the irony of this has not been lost on generations of historians, the fact remained that Mohandas Gandhi, despite his fundamental belief in the doctrinal foundation of the British Empire, found himself a second-class citizen in Natal, and a third-class citizen in Transvaal. The net effect of it was to gall him to remain in South Africa to make a stand on behalf of his people.

The incident that solidified this commitment was a farewell reception held for him by Dada Abdulla, during which discussion centered on a franchise bill currently working its way through the local legislature. The objective of this bill was to remove the rights of Indians to vote. Natal was a self-governing colony, and local elections were for the various seats in the legislature and the office of Prime Minister. By the late 1890s, the Indian population of Natal had grown to the extent that, should Indians take an active interest in politics, the colony would, in effect, become a colony of India. The solution was simply to remove Indians from the ballot, and this was the objective to the new bill. Gandhi, however, found his compatriots apathetic and disinterested. Most were making significant amounts of money through the networks of trade evolving alongside the goldfields, and again, if the price of this was to genuflect in the face of white racism, so be it. Besides this, they asked, who would represent them?

To Gandhi, of course, the answer to this was obvious. He postponed his departure and would remain in South Africa until the eve of World War I, in which time he evolved from a dapper young Indian barrister, dressed in stove-pipe trousers, patent leather shoes and a frock coat, to the *dhoti*-clad mystic purveying his composite religious-political doctrine known as *Satyagraha*. His first task was to compile a petition to be submitted to the office of the Foreign Secretary to protest the discriminatory nature of the Natal Franchise Bill, which required the approval of the Colonial Office before it could take effect in law. The Colonial Secretary was an imperial hawk by the name of Joseph Chamberlain, who studied the proposed legislation, and agreed with the petitioners that it contravened the law and the spirit of the Empire. He did, however, let it be known that if the obviously discriminatory verbiage could be removed from the text, he might be willing to approve it.

The drafting committee then took the document and gave the matter considerable thought. Soon enough, a revised version was returned to the desk of the Colonial Secretary who must have chuckled when he read it at the sheer ingenuity. As qualification for the Natal franchise, an individual was required under the terms of the bill to also enjoy such a right within his home colony. India, of course, was not a self-governing colony, and Indians did not enjoy the right to vote. Chamberlain duly signed the document into law, after which Indians lost their access to the ballot in the British colony of Natal. A letter from Gandhi to Naoroji lamented this state of affairs, illustrating the difference between the spirit of the British imperial charter and its application in the colonies.

Since the colony's black residents were also subjects of her majesty, they were technically entitled to equal access to the franchise of voting, but in practice it was limited by qualification, usually in the form of income, property, and education. On top of this, "natives" were held subject to customary law. This implied that they existed under the jurisdiction of their traditional chiefs, a subordinate and separate system of law. Although the process was long and complicated, and while a few black men did transition from customary to constitutional law, it would be some time before the community as a whole began to take an active interest in politics.

Over the years, Gandhi has actually been condemned as a racist both in South Africa and elsewhere, which is an interesting twist on his legacy. Gandhi almost singlehandedly took on the race policy of South Africa and the British Empire, but he did so with a view to ensuring that Indians were recognized as a "civilized" race and therefore granted a place in the councils of government alongside the whites. At no point did he advocate on behalf of blacks, and on the whole, he seemed to have little to do with the issue of racism against blacks. Indeed, he reformed his Boer War Era ambulance unit during the 1916 Zulu insurrection and took to the field on the side of the British.

In the end, Gandhi would realize that the African Indian struggles were fundamentally different, and that passive resistance was never likely to be a weapon of African revolution. His ambitions did not lie in Africa, but in India, and in 1914, he left South Africa to take up the struggle in the land of his birth.

Equal Rights for all Civilized Men

"The native is to be treated as a child and denied franchise. We must adopt a system of despotism, such as works in India, in our relations with the barbarism of South Africa." – Cecil John Rhodes

In 1652, an advance party of Dutch settlers arrived on the Cape Peninsula to establish a victualing station on behalf of the Dutch East India Company. The early precincts of Cape Town were laid out while in the surrounding countryside gardens, vineyards and orchards were planted. As time passed, and as the early Dutch settlers were augmented by the arrival of French Huguenots, the shoots of a cultured and sophisticated society began to emerge. The territory remained under the administration of a Dutch East India Company "Commander" until 1691 when that role was superseded by a governor, creating from an overseas station a fully constituted colony.

The first governor of the Cape Colony was a professional Dutch colonial administrator by the name of Simon van der Stel, who has been justly credited by history for establishing the traditions of high culture that the Cape is so well known for today. Simon van der Stel was also of mixed race – his mother was Indian – which, ironically, would, in later years, have caused him to be denied access to many of the institutions that he created.

The most interesting story associated with Simon van der Stel is that of his indigenous protégé. The native peoples encountered by these early Dutch settlers were known as "Hottentot," an onomatopoeic term referencing the "click" consonant so characteristic of modern *Khoisan* and southern Bantu languages. As the story goes, Simon van der Stel adopted a Hottentot youth, raising him in his own home, educated him and placed him within the Dutch colonial service. In time, however, the youth returned to the Cape, abandoned the European accoutrements of his "civilization" and returned to his people. It was said that he could be seen from time to time dressed in his loincloth and *kaross* tending to his small herd of sheep.

This story was picked up four decades after Simon van de Stel's death by the French philosopher Jean-Jacques Rousseau and reproduced in his 1755 publication *Discourse on Inequality* to generally illustrate his theory of the "Natural Man." This provoked a great deal of reflection among the thoughts of leaders of the Enlightenment era, who sought to place in the grand order of things the different races of men. In 1795, incidental to the Anglo-French Wars, the British took over the Cape, and the Cape Colony was founded on the very liberal institutions established by Simon van der Stel.

Simon van der Stel

By then British imperial expansion was beginning to directly impact indigenous races from North America to Tasmania, and as time progressed, many within the emerging abolition and aboriginal protection lobby in Britain were beginning to awaken to the problem. In 1837, the Aboriginal Protection Society was founded by a corps of interested parties, included among them Liberal politicians, artists, writers, explorers and missionaries. One of them was abolitionist and parliamentarian Sir Thomas Fowell Buxton, who sat on the chair of a parliamentary select committee authorized to investigate the condition of aboriginal peoples in the colonies. This marked an important moment in the development of an imperial contract, and the preamble to the report details the mandate of the inquiry: "[To] consider what measures ought to be adopted with regards to the native inhabitants of the countries where British settlements are made, and to the neighbouring tribes, in order to secure to them the due observance of justice, and the protection of their rights; to promote the spread of civilisation among them, and to lead them to the peaceful and voluntary reception of the Christian religion."

Sir Fowell Buxton

The report spoke to all of the major settled colonies of the Empire: Canada, New Zealand, Australia and of course South Africa. It spoke also from the vantage of British global predominance but underlined at the same time the responsibility felt by the British people to balance their global ambitions with the humane usage of the Empire's aboriginal peoples.

While few of the British Overseas Territories took any of this particularly seriously, the Cape Colony was certainly one that did. In 1853, the Cape was granted a representative government which, although it did not remove the colony from the umbrella of the imperial government, it allowed it to form its own parliament and to draft and adopt a constitution. Enshrined in that constitution was the guarantee of a multi-racial franchise, something required by British imperial law and convention, but rarely enforced, and which, in this case, tended to reflect a colonial leadership determined to make real a truly egalitarian and colourless society.

In reality, in the early days, indigenous people's access to the franchise was limited by property and education qualifications, as well as the tendency of native people to stick to traditional lifestyles. However, as missionary education in the Eastern Cape drove up levels of literacy, political awareness began to spread, until, in due course, the black vote became a vital factor in local parliamentary elections. A succession of liberal governors encouraged the development of a native press and black political associations while at the same time defending this rather unique state of affairs against attacks from other British colonies. In 1872, the colony became self-governing, and Prime Minister John Molteno, along with his daughter Elizabeth, led the liberal movement in the Cape, fiercely protective of what was in real terms a unique experiment in race relations. In defence of this policy, contemporary parliamentarian William Porter issued what would prove to be an extremely prophetic warning. "Why should you fear the exercise of franchise?" he asked. "This is a delicate question, but it must be touched upon. I do not hesitate to say that I would rather meet the Hottentot at the hustings, voting for his representative, than in the wilds with his gun upon his shoulder. Is it not better to disarm them by granting them the privileges of the constitution? If you now blast all their hopes and tell them they shall not fight their battles constitutionally, do not you yourselves apply to them the stimulus to fight their battles unconstitutionally?"[1]

---

[1] William Porter, Cape Colony Legislative Council, March 9, 1852.

"Christianity and Commerce" and the "Sacred Trust"

"The strangest disease I have seen in this country seems really to be broken-heartedness, and it attacks free men who have been captured and made slaves." – Dr. David Livingstone

One of the most famous Britons of the late 19th century was Dr. David Livingstone, whose expeditions in Africa are among the most renowned. His ideology in the era of the anti-slavery movement in Africa was "Christianity and Commerce." Full abolition was made law throughout the British Empire in 1833, and this sounded the death knell of the Transatlantic Slave Trade, which would limp along under Portuguese control until about 1850 when the importation of African slaves in Brazil was finally halted. However, the East African Slave Trade continued until at least 1873, when it too was brought to an end by a British treaty cosigned by the Sultan of Zanzibar.

Livingstone

Livingstone, who incidentally died that same year, dedicated his life to the suppression of this most violent and pernicious traffic, and his solution to the proliferation of slavery in east and central Africa was the introduction of Christian missionaries to banish the darkness of pagan idolatry and legitimate trade and commerce to oust the illicit trade in slaves. Christianity and Commerce. The idea gained currency and became in many respects a slogan for the imperial movement of the late 19th century known as "The Scramble for Africa." The "Scramble" was, of course, premised far more on the rise of capital and industry in Europe than any particular regard for Africans' suffering; after all, Africa offered fresh markets for European manufactured goods and new reserves of raw materialss. However, the rise of a humanitarian movement in Britain during and after the abolition campaign demanded that the new imperial charter emphasize the upliftment of the native African from his debased state to a full and equal place under the sun. Cecil John Rhodes, the most notorious British capital imperialist, offered up a formula for imperialism in the late 19th century as "Philanthropy plus five per cent." This certainly put matters in perspective.

Rhodes

"Christianity and Commerce" thus came to define an era which was, in practical terms, an effort to stamp out the embers of slavery and utilize the benign elements of European imperialism to protect and uplift a race of people on many fronts destroyed by the horrors of European slavery. While the irony and hypocrisy of this have not been lost on generations of modern historians, and while a great many other motives superseded any real concern for the well-being of indigenous Africans, this, nonetheless, was the moral principle upon which colonization in Africa proceeded.

By then, the Royal Proclamation of 1858 had already established the principle of absolute equality among all of Her Majesty's overseas subjects, regardless of race, color, or religion. While the type of tampering that would remove the Indians from the Natal electorate would be replicated all over the English-speaking world, as the British Empire spread during the late 19th century, hundreds of new territories came under British "protection," subjecting their indigenous populations to the sovereignty of the British Crown. During the era of "Christianity and Commerce," the political rights of indigenous people were typically signed away by traditional rulers enticed by guns and liquor, committing their seals to documents the implications of which they had absolutely idea.

The ultimate result, as history will attest, was the almost absolute European takeover of Africa by the closing decade of the 19th century. At the same time, by the 1890s, thanks to the efforts of missionary involvement in Africa, educated youth were at last beginning to awaken to the opportunities and limitations of European imperialism. In the Cape, a sizable black electorate began utilizing the vote, forming their own organizations and pressure groups, and publishing their own newspapers, pamphlets, and manifestos. This, at least in the early days, was encouraged by colonial authorities.

The British Empire in Africa was not monolithic, so different territories had different characteristics that required different political approaches. In general, however, the empire could be divided into two types of colony: those such as Australia, New Zealand, Canada and South Africa with climates and economies conducive to large scale European settlement, and those like Nigeria that were not. The leading personality in the Cape as the century drew to a close was Rhodes, while the man at the wheel of affairs in Nigeria was the influential explorer, soldier and imperial administrator Lord Frederick Lugard. Each man according to his particular circumstances sought to devise a formula to transition colonial rule from the era of Christianity and Commerce to that which became known as the "Sacred Trust." There is a certain weary inevitability in the fact that, while in the Cape an open door was promised, that door was bolted evermore tightly as blacks began to increasingly knock upon it. In 1890, Rhodes was elected to the office of Prime Minister of the Cape Colony, and his view of the racial landscape was defined by himself as "equal rights for all civilized men." In 1894 he piloted through the Cape parliament an article of legislation known as the "Glen Grey Act" which sought, on many fronts, to limit black access to the franchise through increased qualifications and the removal of communally owned land as a property qualification. The Glen Grey Act, which was ostensibly experimental by being confined to a region of the Eastern Cape known as Glen Grey, also contained new rules of taxation designed to coax those living under communal conditions away from the land and into the growing labor market by the requirement placed on a head of household to earn cash. This, it was hoped, would jumpstart a consumer society, which would, in turn, form the bedrock of a black, urban working class to support predominately white mining, agriculture, and industry.

Lugard

The Glen Grey Act in and of itself did not alter the political landscape much, but it established an attitude that grew in influence in the Cape that black access to the vote was not a useful liberty. Rhodes' successor, John Merriman, spoke for a growing minority when he said, "I do not like the natives at all, and I wish that we had no black man in South Africa. But there they are, and our lot is cast with them by an overruling providence and the only question is how to shape our course so as to maintain the supremacy of our race and at the same time do our duty."

Although wary of its potential to flood the electorate with non-white voters, Merriman advocated the Cape electoral system as a safety valve, which, as he observed, although noisy and potentially troublesome, was nonetheless the safest contingency against an explosion. In defense of equal rights to voting stood a strong lobby of liberals, led by the indefatigable civil rights

activist Olive Schreiner, and backed up by her brother Philip and the likes of Gandhi, among
others.

Schreiner

Meanwhile, things were very different in Nigeria. Frederick Lugard had only to worry about
the few white expatriates who staffed the administration and managed local, British-owned
businesses. There would never be a problem of white settlement in such an uncomfortable
climate as the Niger Delta. It was Lugard, however, who piloted the colony from a largely
corporate owned entity to a full British overseas dependency, encompassing the two separate
protectorates of Southern and Northern Nigeria. It is perhaps incidental that Lugard has been
judged poorly by history for a signature blunder committed in 1914, which was to combine the
two protectorates into one. In this way was established the British colony of Nigeria, which
attempted to create a cultural assimilation out of the disparate elements of the Christian-animist
south and the Islamic north.

The emirates and sultanates of the north possessed ancient traditions of administration that
deeply impressed Lugard, who, in common with most British imperialists of the era, tended to be
inspired by ancient, ruling aristocracies. From this emerged his signature theory of "Indirect
Rule," under which the colonial government tended to be characterized by a political agent,
usually a district or provincial commissioner. This political agent acted only in an advisory role,
very rarely extending to a supervisory role, making use of established institutions to continue the

government of an ancient kingdom with nothing more than very minor modifications. Those modifications tended to be limited to law, taxation and the outlawing of slavery. The overall objective, besides husbanding meagre administrative resources, was to refashion such ancient systems of government in such a way that they might function in modern, political and diplomatic terms, preparing the ground for inevitable independence. Lugard referred to this as the Dual Mandate, and it was later referred to in the Covenant of the League of Nations as the Sacred Trust.

The Sacred Trust thereafter became something of an article of faith when it came to imperialists' view of African colonization. The racial contretemps triggered in South Africa by Gandhi and his *Satyagraha* movement set off a similar series of protests on the part of the Indian communities of East Africa. Given the voices in India pushing for independence, the British government was unwilling to either encourage or put down the movements with any severity. In a 1923 parliamentary debate over the matter, Victor Cavendish, then Colonial Secretary, made these remarks: "Primarily Kenya is an African territory, and His Majesty's Government think it necessary definitely to record their considered opinion that the interests of the African natives must be paramount and that if, and when, those interests and the interests of the immigrant races should conflict, the former should prevail. Obviously, the interests of the other communities, European, Indian or Arab, must severally be safeguarded, but in the administration of Kenya, His Majesty's Government regard themselves as exercising a trust on behalf of the African population, and they are unable to delegate or share this trust, the object of which may be defined as the protection and advancement of the native races." This was the Sacred Trust in a nutshell, and while Lord Frederick Lugard, by then serving on the Mandate Commission of the League of Nations, would have agreed wholeheartedly, Cecil John Rhodes would have turned in his grave.

Cavendish

Not ssurprisingly, it was South African race policy in the aftermath of the Boer War that most severely challenged the Sacred Trust and British stewardship of it. The Boer War was a final reckoning between the British and Boer in South Africa. South Africa, with its vital strategic location and staggering mineral wealth, was something the British were not prepared to sacrifice to the Boer, who had German sympathies and affiliations, and as the 19th century closed, years of diplomatic jostling and neighborly hostility ended in war. The British Empire prevailed, but on the eve then of World war I, the British needed the loyalty of all dominions and colonies, so the British imperial government was prepared to overlook all of its lofty principles in the interests of satisfying a violently racist and xenophobic Boer population via the formation of the Union of South Africa.

In the negotiations between the four territories that made up British South Africa to unify as a single dominion, the most difficult issue was reconciling wildly divergent race policies. The Cape held on with valiant determination to its color-blind franchise while the Transvaal and Orange River Colonies pressed for the complete disenfranchisement of the non-white races and their removal from cities and all viable land. In the end, the constitution of the Union of South Africa, ratified by an act of the British Parliament, allowed for the continuation of the Cape system of franchise at a local, provincial level, but gave it no national reach, meaning that black representation on the central legislature of the new Dominion of South Africa would be in the form of appointed white members with responsibility for black affairs. As a result, while the British increasingly withdrew from direct involvement in South African affairs, discriminatory legislation steadily invaded the statute, eroding the effectiveness of the Cape system. In the aftermath of WWII, the solidification of apartheid took hold as a statutory race doctrine, and non-whites in the Cape lost their access to the vote altogether.

The Yellow Peril

"We are guarding the last part of the world in which the higher races can live and increase freely for the higher civilization." – Charles H. Pearson

The foundation of the large South African Indian community that Gandhi worked on behalf of could be traced to the late 19th century institution of indentured labor, which was devised and implemented in response to the labor crisis occasioned by the abolition of the slave trade. Through this system, many thousands of low-caste, impoverished Indians were recruited for service overseas, very few of whom availed themselves of the mandatory facility of return at the end of their contractual term. As noted earlier, the unrestricted influx of Indians into South Africa, an already incendiary race environment, created enormous discomfort. So serious, indeed, was the anti-Indian sentiment in South Africa that, in the aftermath of the Boer War, with British priorities being the resumption of the mining industry on the Witwatersrand, the colonial authorities did not dare suggest the importation of Indian labor.[2] It was decided instead to import Chinese labor under similar terms, which prompted an immediate and violent backlash from white labor, which spilt over into a mass movement in Britain in support of white labor in South Africa. The essential grievance was xenophobic, insofar as the Boer War had been fought to secure South Africa as a British economic asset, and by extension to create opportunities for British labor and capital, which the importation of Chinese labor did not appear to support. Nonetheless, a shipment of Chinese workers was imported and set to work in the mines. They were greeted with such hostility, and their experience was so uncomfortable, that, despite heartfelt appeals from their leaders, they were eventually sent home again.

The lesson learned by this experiment was learned well, and Chinese labor did not feature to any great extent in South Africa. Chinese labor, however, did find its way into the United States, employed particularly in railway construction, as well as in Canada and Australia to support the various mining sectors. It was in Australia, located in the Asia-Pacific region, that fear of the "Yellow Peril" took root most securely, resulting in the "White Australia" policy that specifically

---

[2] The British Expeditionary Force that fought the Boer during the Anglo Boer War made extensive use of black labor for the multitude of basic labor requirements necessary to keep an army of some 200,000 men in the field, offering high wages that, in the immediate aftermath of the war, disinclined most to then seek work underground in the gold mines.

aimed to restrict the influx of "Chinese, Hindoos and men of other Eastern races." The "White Australia" policy was manifest in the Immigration Restriction Act of 1901, which sought to reconcile a federation-wide system of Asian exclusion with the established British imperial policy defined in the Royal Proclamation of 1858.

The discovery of gold in Australia in 1851 triggered a gold rush, which in turn led to a sudden influx of immigrants from all over the world, most from European countries, but also, over the course of the next 20 years, some 50,000 Chinese, mostly Cantonese. These men and women were not introduced as bonded labor, as they were in the mines of the Witwatersrand, but participated in the gold rush as independent prospectors, achieving success in many instances and accumulating significant wealth. They also reaped fortunes in business and trade on the fringes of the bonanza, generally attracting the animus of the predominantly white mining class. This prompted several significant protests and riots. A commission of inquiry was appointed to the goldfields of Victoria to gather evidence about the grievances and problems of the miners. This led to legal restrictions placed on the immigration of Chinese into both Victoria and New South Wales, with additional residency tax levies on the Chinese.

Besides expressing irritation at Chinese competition in the goldfields, there was a more subliminal sense within the combined colonies that unrestricted Chinese immigration would inevitably overwhelm the relatively sparse population of Europeans. Anti-Chinese sentiment was abundantly reflected in Australian popular culture, stereotyping the Chinese as insidious and invasive and a threat to the sanctity of Anglo-Saxon culture in Australia. However, restrictions placed on Chinese immigration in individual colonies was easily circumvented by simply entering the continent in a colony with low Chinese immigration and traveling overland to the goldfields. It would be almost 30 years before inter-territorial cooperation would solidify to the point that a common immigration policy was implemented.

By the end of the 1880s, the British became aware of moves within Australia to enact a highly restrictive, continent-wide policy limiting non-white immigration, and the government was obligated for the sake of its imperial charter to sound a note of caution. While Colonial Secretary Lord Knutsford was apt to express sympathy for the colonists, acknowledging their right to control their domestic affairs, he urged that they approach the matter with due respect for British imperial and diplomatic sensitivities. It stood against the British imperial charter to explicitly exclude any immigrant to any colony based on ethnicity or race. To specifically target the Chinese in this regard held the potential to offend the Qing government and the Chinese people, British diplomatic allies, and expanding this to include Japanese and Indian immigrants ran entirely roughshod over British overseas interests. Calls for restraint were taken up by the India and Colonial Offices in Whitehall, by the Viceroy of India himself, and by the Japanese diplomatic legations in each of the Australians colonies. Joseph Chamberlain, Secretary of State for the Colonies from 1895-1903, suggested to the various Australian premiers that they consider the so-called "Natal formula" in devising their own common immigration policy. Chamberlain had signed into law the Natal Franchise Act, and the key element of the Natal formula was a literacy test that obliged Indian and Oriental arrivals in the colony – generally classified as "Asiatics" – to prove their proficiency in a European language. This test required that they dictate and write a passage either in English, French, German, Dutch or Yiddish, and if they failed, they were denied a certificate of entry. This obviously offered the potential for the selective acceptance of immigrants based on race while at the same time mitigating the unseemly insensitivities of local prejudice.

Chamberlain

The first sitting of the Australian federal parliament easily achieved consensus that unrestricted Asian immigration would be disastrous to a self-governing colony founded on the principles of white political and economic citizenship. In response to British anxieties, it was stated simply that the empire would ultimately benefit from a racially heterogenous Australia. The debate, therefore, centered not on whether to restrict Asian immigration, but how best to achieve it. On one side was the argument in favor of the Natal Formula and on the other immigration restrictions purely on the grounds of race.

The Immigration Restriction Bill was introduced to Parliament on August 7, 1901, and most reluctantly the Natal Formula was adopted. Royal assent was required for any homegrown legislation to be adopted into law, and clearly, a race-specific immigration exclusion policy would never survive scrutiny by the Colonial Office. The moral justification for the Immigration Restriction Act when it finally became law was the simple reality that Australia's vulnerable and exposed position in the South Pacific region justified more strenuous efforts than any other dominion in limiting the influx of non-whites. If Australia was overrun by Indians or Chinese, then Australia would be lost to the British Empire, and notwithstanding all the lofty language of empire solidarity, of equality and impartiality enshrined in the imperial charter, few in the British imperial establishment did not acknowledge the truth of this. Labour Party leader King O'Malley, American by birth, aired an opinion very well received on both the front and backbenches of the Australian Federal Parliament: "If the Australian people had only lived in the Southern states of America, as I have, and had seen the dire results of the present mingling of the Africans with the whites, they would put their feet down and say, 'We are going to profit by the terrible mistake of the American people, and we are not going to leave it to posterity to solve such an unholy problem.'"

O'Malley

On September 6, 1901, the deputy leader of the Free Trade Party, Sir William McMillan, uttered a similar sentiment, effectively closing the book on the debate: "I hold that if we are perfectly sure that a certain policy is necessary to uphold the purity of the race in Australia…I do not think we should hesitate, for one moment, under the peculiar circumstances of the case – with our position in these southeastern seas, open to millions of these servile and alien people – to say to Great Britain, 'This is a problem which you and we have to face, and the more honestly we face it the better for the future.'"

The 1901 Immigration Restriction Act was not the only legal instrument of its type to be enacted within the geographic scope of the British Empire. There was, of course, not only the 1897 Natal Immigration Restriction Act, wherein the "Natal Formula" was cast into law, but also the much more specific Canadian Chinese Immigration Acts of 1885 and 1923. The first of these framed around the 1882 Chinese Exclusion Act which placed a prohibition on all Chinese immigration into the United States. The 1885 Act imposed a $50 head tax on all Chinese entering Canada, according to the recommendations of a Royal Commission on Chinese Immigration of the same year, authorized by Canadian Prime Minister Sir John A. Macdonald.

As was the case in the United States, the Chinese arrived in Canada primarily as labor for the construction of the Canadian Pacific Railway, with most coming from China, but many also from the United States. In an environment of rapid development and shortages of labor, they were initially welcomed, but as the need for cheap labor diminished, a fear took root that Chinese were in some way a threat to Canadian jobs. There was also, as was the case in Australia, a visceral fear and distrust of an alien culture, and with the almost unlimited potential for immigration, a sense of imminent peril that white predominance in British North America would be inevitably compromised. The 1923 Chinese Immigration Act, one of the last and most explicit pieces of legislation of its type, added to existing legislation by not merely discouraging Chinese immigration through uneven taxation, but restricting arrivals to diplomats, students, merchants and any other "special circumstance" as approved by the Minister of Immigration.

Interestingly, the 1923 Act did not only include Chinese from China and the United States, but those holding British nationality. The act was repealed only in 1947 as Canada became a signatory to the United Nations Declaration of Human Rights, replaced in general terms by the Canadian Citizenship Act of 1946.

The Windrush Generation

"England lay before us, not as a place or a people, but as a promise and an expectation." – George Lamming

The corner of the British Empire that benefitted most from abolition was the Caribbean. Slavery was abolished in the British West Indies in 1838, after a four-year period, colloquially known as "apprenticeship," in which slaves were paid wages. The societies and economies of the

British West Indies, Jamaica in particular, were established around the industrial production of sugar, rum and molasses, and were as a consequence developed to an extent more commonly associated with the dominions. A class of free blacks existed, involved in commerce and trade, while many who were technically slaves did likewise by paying a prescribed stipend to their owners for the privilege. Therefore, abolition found the country and society of the British West Indies, Jamaica in particular, in a relatively advanced state, especially compared to such places as Haiti and the Dominican Republic, which existed in a state of very low development.

Abolition was not a state of affairs imposed on a reluctant British public, but rather the culmination of a growing humanitarian movement as noted above. The British Empire was evolving into something larger and more beneficial than simply an economic network of colonies and plantation islands run for the sole purpose of generating profit. The architects of the modern imperial charter, echoed in many other European capitals, established the theory of the "civilizing" mission of empire, a sacred duty to uplift the diversity of indigenous people under British protection to a place of equality with themselves. Aboriginal culture had little value itself, besides as an anthropological curiosity, but simply morally deficient in the absence of Christianity, modern education and labor. The provision of these, at least in theory, provided the moral foundation of the European takeover of so much of the earth's surface, the belief that the native peoples of the world only need feel the warmth of Anglo-Saxon civilization to unfurl, embrace the light and multiply.

While, as history has tended to prove, these lofty principles seldom translated into positive action and were often further complicated by the internal politics of colonies and dominions, they underwrote a great deal of effort in the Caribbean to provide the means of creating citizens out of a population of emancipated slaves. A primary education system was established, and as the payment of wages translated into capital and spending, banks sprung up alongside widespread experimentation with industrial machinery to streamline production and introduce new skills and new commodities. Names like Marcus Garvey began to circulate against a backdrop of Negritude and the Harlem Renaissance, and the British West Indies entered the modern era conspicuously less disadvantaged than many other parts of the Caribbean.

A highly stratified society remained in place, broadly characterized by race, and within the confines of island communities, each with already unsustainable populations, there was a limit to what standards of development could be achieved by a majority of poor urban and rural blacks. That said, as the 20th century dawned, all of the islands of the British West Indians enjoyed high levels of literacy and an elite class of well educated people among the population. Given the local unemployment or underemployment, emigration became frequent.

For the first half of the 20th century, as the pace of Jamaican emigration gradually gathered, destinations tended to be local, including to the South and North American mainland and other Caribbean islands such as Cuba. Very little direct communication in this regard took place between the British West Indies and the British mainland, which was extraordinarily distant, and this remained the case until World War II. During the war, significant numbers of West Indian servicemen found their way to the British, establishing contacts and relationships, with a handful remaining behind.

More significantly, as post-war Europe lay in ruins, Labour-led Britain faced the daunting task of rebuilding with a diminished labor market, exacerbated by a wave of outbound emigration of demobilized servicemen and their families to the colonies. This left a significant hole in the metropolitan labor force, especially as women and retirees left the jobs that they had held during the war as part of the wider war effort. India, Pakistan, and Ceylon achieved independence, which set in motion a domino effect that began the wider process of decolonization. Since no specific law existed in Britain to control or limit the movement of people between the colonies themselves, or between the colonies and mainland Britain, as those colonies became independent nation-states, this clearly had to change.

In 1946, the Canadian Citizenship Act was passed, creating the unique and separate status of "Canadian Citizen." This prompted the convening of a Commonwealth Conference in London the following year, during which it was agreed that each Commonwealth member state would be free to similarly legislate on behalf of its own citizens without compromising the integral structure of the Commonwealth itself. This, in effect, was the devolution of the empire from a whole to a constellation of separate parts. The net result was the British Nationality Act of 1948, then Australia's Nationality and Citizenship Act of 1948, New Zealand's British Nationality and New Zealand Citizenship Act of 1948, and Southern Rhodesia's Southern Rhodesian Citizenship and British Nationality Act of 1949. The British Nationality Act defined the new status of "citizen of the United Kingdom and Colonies," which included people either born or naturalized in the United Kingdom itself or any one of its overseas colonies.

What this meant for British West Indians, in respect of emigration, was that Britain became the only developed overseas country where entry was not controlled at arrival.[3] Interestingly, the British Nationality Act received Royal assent on July 31, 1948, a month after the *Empire Windrush* drew up alongside the Tilbury docks. While most historians tend to mark this up as purely coincidental, and it appears that British authorities were taken by surprise at the sudden arrival of so many West Indians, the terms of the 1948 Act left the door wide open for the waves of non-white Commonwealth immigrants that followed from the Caribbean.

With the benefit of hindsight, the Act was extraordinary liberal, awarding equal status in law to everyone born within the British Empire in any part of the world. In the words of Lord Chancellor William Allen Jowitt, "We can say that people come from one part of the British Empire shall not be allowed in and people from another part shall be allowed in, but in this great

---

[3] The US Immigration Act of 1924, or Johnson–Reed Act, which including the Asian Exclusion Act and National Origins Act, effectively blocked the entry of black West Indians into the United States.

metropolitan center of the Empire I hope we never shall say such a thing."

Arguably, these sentiments were expressed entirely in the absence of any expectation that large numbers of New Commonwealth citizens would be tempted to exercise their right to permanently reside in the United Kingdom, and there certainly was no verbiage in any of the debates to suggest that anyone conceived of such a thing. Some one billion members of the Commonwealth potentially enjoyed this right, although before the promulgation of the Act only small numbers of imperial subjects had ever immigrated permanently to the United Kingdom, and a majority of these were white, with those non-whites tending mainly to be Indians.

It did not take long for this open-armed and benevolent attitude to begin to fray, with anxious press utterances and parliamentary debate mentioning the first expressions of popular disquiet at the numbers of non-white immigrants appearing on the streets and in the workforce. The liberal Labor Prime Minister Clement Attlee attempted to soothe Parliament by reminding members, "It is traditional that British subjects, whether of Dominion or Colonial origin (and of whatever race or colour) should be freely admissible to the United Kingdom…That tradition is not, in my view, to be lightly discarded…If our policy were to result in a great influx of undesirables, we might, however unwillingly, have to consider modifying it."

Nonetheless, the passengers of the *Empire Windrush* and other ships that followed arrived and filtered into the labor market, taking advantage of their free right of entry and abode with very little if any documentation supporting their entry and settlement.[4] Many arrived having left families behind, some never to be seen again, and others brought over relatives as soon as the breadwinner was settled. While the *Empire Windrush* lent its name to the wider movement of black West Indians to Britain, it was only the first of many - between 1948 and 1971, an estimated 600,000 people made that crossing, and they are now known as the *Windrush Generation.*

By the early 1950s, as the immediate post-war labor crisis eased, expressions of disquiet began to be increasingly heard in media, popular culture, and Parliamentary debates. Before World War II, British society was largely homogenous, and its imperial complexion was visible only in the various universities where minority students studied, as well as in a few urban pockets. By the end of the 1950s, on the other hand, entire urban neighborhoods were dominated by immigrants, and the trend was growing. Throughout the 1950s and early 1960s, the sheer number of agonized Parliamentary debates, centered on limiting the flow of economic migrants, revealed the clear dichotomy between the government's publicly expressed support of the movement and its unspoken regret and hostility. The essence of the debates was whether to introduce immigration controls to all Commonwealth citizens, which would affect whites as well as non-whites, or to hide discriminatory deportation and limitations behind a general ordinance to remove and bar entry to "riff-raff" from overseas.

---

[4] Major recruiters were the various borough and city public transport agencies, the Royal Mail and the newly established National Health Service.

In the autumn of 1958, a sense of urgency was injected into the issue through a series of race riots that broke out in the London borough of Notting Hill, followed by another in the Midlands city of Nottingham, and other less volatile instances scattered across the urban and industrial landscape of England. By then, black economic migration was not the only visible phenomenon; Indians, Bangladeshis and Pakistanis were arriving in increasing numbers, as were Chinese from Hong Kong and a growing number of black Africans. Significant opposition was finding expression in such quarters as the Monday Club, a Conservative pressure group whose Members of Parliament were active and vocal in their opposition to what was increasingly manifest as a movement of mass immigration.

It all culminated in the promulgation of the Commonwealth Immigrants Act of 1962, which, for the first time, racialized the term "immigrant." The door to entry and settlement was now closed to all but those Commonwealth citizens born in the United Kingdom or the Republic of Ireland, or those who held British passports. A system of vouchers was introduced to deal with those entering the United Kingdom to fill local labor requirements, or those seeking education. Thus, for the first time, Commonwealth citizens found themselves subject to the same conditions of entry and limitations as non-Commonwealth citizens, which was an obvious reversal of the original spirit of the Commonwealth, but was also widely seen as an inevitable requirement in the face of mass immigration and a rising upswell of popular discontent and racial tension. There was an understanding that those already in the country who had been permanently domiciled for more than five years enjoyed the implicit right to remain. However, another important point is that little if any documentation was issued to support this, which would have bitter ramifications in the years to come.

In the meantime, the unofficial voice of the anti-immigration lobby was Enoch Powell, Conservative MP for Wolverhampton South West, who rose to prominence on the back of what has since become an iconic speech delivered to a General Meeting of the West Midlands Area Conservative Political Centre. In his "Rivers of Blood" speech, he said in part, "As I look ahead, I am filled with foreboding. Like the Roman, I seem to see 'the River Tiber foaming with much blood.' That tragic and intractable phenomenon which we watch with horror on the other side of the Atlantic but which there is interwoven with the history and existence of the States itself, is coming upon us here by our own volition and our own neglect. Indeed, it has all but come. In numerical terms, it will be of American proportions long before the end of the century. Only resolute and urgent action will avert it even now. Whether there will be the public will to demand and obtain that action, I do not know. All I know is that to see, and not to speak, would be the great betrayal."

Allan Warren's portrait of Powell

Then, in 1968, as large numbers of Kenyan Indians were leaving the former colony of Kenya for Britain in the face of a general policy of open discrimination against Indians, a hasty revision of the 1962 statute resulted in the Commonwealth Immigrants Act of 1968. This further restricted entry into the United Kingdom, barring all except those who could prove the birth of a father or grandfather in Britain. This obviously favored white Commonwealth citizens, and few Indians and blacks could offer such proof.

In tandem with all of this came the various Race Relations Acts, the first in 1965, the second in 1968, and the third in 1976, which outlawed all expressions of racial discrimination, serving as an admission that such practices were widespread throughout the kingdom.

Then came the Immigration Act of 1971, which brought the status of Commonwealth citizens into line with aliens and introduced a raft of measures to facilitate detention and deportation of foreign nationals. The terms now adopted were "patrial" and "non-patrial," effectively ending the right of non-white Commonwealth citizens to migrate and settle in the United Kingdom. With regards to those already resident in the United Kingdom, the statute considered a person to have the right of abode in the United Kingdom if "he is a citizen of the United Kingdom and Colonies who has at any time been settled in the United Kingdom and Islands and had at that time (and while such a citizen) been ordinarily resident there for the last five years or more."

The Windrush Scandal

"We can deport first and hear appeals later." – Theresa May

Arguably the most emotive issue in the European Union is immigration. Within 50 years of the docking of the *Empire Windrush,* immigration into the United Kingdom had morphed from a novelty to a political crisis, promoting the first discussions of British separation from the European Union and compelling the government to adopt increasingly desperate and draconian measures. The British public, which by the start of the 21st century was one of most internationally diverse in the world, had mixed feelings about immigration. On the one hand, the country celebrated its diversity, its liberalism, and its tradition of offering asylum, but on the other, the burden placed on social services and the British taxpayer was proving untenable. The sheer volume of people entering and attempting to enter Britain illegally, thereafter to claim asylum and/or failing to leave if rejected, prompted what came to be known as the "hostile environment" policy.

This policy, in the briefest terms, was a Home Office creation, devised by then Home Secretary Theresa May, to make it as difficult as possible for those without recourse to remain, in the hope, no doubt, that they would simply leave voluntarily. There were many facets to this policy, but in essence, the Immigration Acts of 2014 and 2016 were to be rigorously enforced, shutting out those illegally in the country from social benefits, the ability to rent accommodation, the ability to acquire a driver's license, and access to the National Health. The policy also led to a more complicated and costly application process to acquire leave to remain.

The Windrush Generation and their children found themselves in many instances being treated as illegal immigrants. The effect of this was to abruptly cut off long-term residents of the United Kingdom, in particular older members of the Windrush Generation, from access to social and health services, housing, and jobs. Many of these older residents had arrived in the country during the chaotic and unregulated early days and had never acquired documentation, and they had never found it necessary to apply for a passport. Thousands of letters sent out by a Home Office contractor were received by members of the Windrush Generation, and the letters instructed them that they had no legal right to be in the United Kingdom. Quite a number left of their own accord, others were deported, and yet others sought at the last minute to navigate the complexities of applying for leave to remain. Some of these individuals were people who were born in the United Kingdom and had never left.

This situation continued largely unreported upon from the implementation of the Hostile Environment policy through the end of 2017, when press reports began to circulate detailing Home Office efforts to deport people who had arrived in the United Kingdom before 1973 if they were unable to prove their right to remain. It has been estimated by the Migration Observatory at the University of Oxford that as many as 57,000 people were affected, with only 15,000 of those represented by the Windrush Generation, so the term "Windrush Scandal" is rather general. Many others from numerous Commonwealth countries were also caught up in the dragnet. The government was accused of a "deport now ask questions later," which was certainly true. Indeed, there seems to have been no particular effort to hide it.

By the spring of 2018, questions were beginning to be asked in Parliament, and very quickly the issue exploded into a full-blown political scandal. Theresa May had since become Prime Minister of Great Britain, and Amber Rudd was the Secretary for Home Affairs. Significance of documentation was found to have either been lost or destroyed, and while their applications were under consideration, elderly residents were denied health services, cut off from their bank accounts, prohibited from renting accommodation, and not allowed to work. The Home Office was accused of being in full knowledge of the effects of all of this, and perhaps inevitably, due to the disproportionate number of older, black residents affected, the episode was framed as an example of the systemic nature of racism in Great Britain.

While it may be that racism did not player a greater role than ineptitude and bureaucratic blindness, the issue reverberated through a society sensitive to such issues with ferocity. In conformity to targets and official recommendation, a great deal of passion was applied to the issue, in particular in the run-up to the 2018 general election when immigration was a live issue. In April 2018, British Home Secretary Amber Rudd resigned, admitting that she had "inadvertently misled the Home Affairs Committee." Numerous Parliamentary committees were convened and gathered evidence, and the matter was deeply studied and reported upon. Several official apologies were offered, and the press championed the cause of those affected, deported, and rendered destitute by the entire episode, noting little if any real attempt to provide redress. Deportations were halted, application fees waived, and other demonstrative efforts made, but the damage was done, and more importantly, no one really knew the full extent of the fallout, so what ultimately could be remedied was limited.

The Windrush Scandal in many respects marked the end of a chapter of imperial migration to Britain, and the love-hate relationship this erstwhile colonizing power now has with the millions of people and their descendants who at one time were subjects of the British Crown. In the age of globalization and mass immigration, this remains as uncomfortable a responsibility as it was when the gangplank of the *Empire Windrush* landed with a clang on British shores and the first members of the Windrush Generation stepped ashore to greet their sovereign motherland.